So Many Bunnies

a bedtime abc

and counting

book

SO MANY BUNNIES

a b e d t i m e   a b c

and counting book

Rick Walton ✆ Paige Miglio

SCHOLASTIC INC.
New York Toronto London Auckland Sydney
Mexico City New Delhi Hong Kong

Old Mother Rabbit lived in a shoe.
She had twenty-six children and knew what to do.
She fed them some carrots, some broth, and some bread,
Then kissed them all gently and put them to bed.

1 was named Abel.
He slept on the table.

2 was named **B**lair.
She slept in a chair.

4 was named Dee.
She slept in a tree.

3 was named Carol.
She slept in a barrel.

5 was named Ellis.
He slept on the trellis.

6 was named Frankie.
She slept on a hankie.

7 was named Gretel.
She slept in the kettle.

8 was named Hank.
He slept with his bank.

9 was named Ike.
He slept on his trike.

10 was named Jane.
She slept in the lane.

11 was named **K**ate.
She slept on the gate.

12 was named Link.
He slept in the sink.

13 was named **M**andy.
She slept in the candy.

14 was named **N**oel.
He slept in a bowl.

15 was named **O**llie.
He slept by the holly.

16 was named Pat.
She slept in a hat.

17 was named **Q**uinn.
He slept in a bin.

18 was named Rae.
She slept in the hay.

19 was named **S**am.
He slept with his lamb.

20 was named Toni.
She slept with her pony.

21 was named **U**te.
He slept by the fruit.

22 was named **V**ern.
He slept by a fern.

23 was named **W**illow.
She slept on a pillow.

24 was named **X**en.
He slept with his pen.

25 was named **Y**ale.
He slept by the scale.

26 was named Zed.
He slept on the shed.

Old Mother Rabbit lived in a shoe.
She had twenty-six children and plenty to do.
She tucked them all in, from Abel to Zed,
Then curled herself up in a soft feather bed.

To Evan and Betty Jo Ivie, who had many children and knew what to do.
—RW

To my baby bunny, Marcus, and his brothers Nathan and Noel and Jeremy.
And to the "Mother Bunny," Judy Sue.
—PM

Pen-and-ink over watercolors was used for the full-color illustrations. The text type is 24-point Powell Old Style.

ISBN 0-439-07775-3

12 11 10 9 8 7 6 5 4 3 2 1   9/9 0 1 2 3 4/0

Printed in the U.S.A   14

First Scholastic printing, September 1998